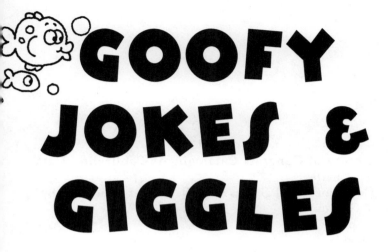

GOOFY JOKES & GIGGLES

CHARLES KELLER

Illustrated by Dave Garbot

Sterling Publishing Co., Inc.
New York

Library of Congress Cataloging-in-Publication Data
Keller, Charles.
  Goofy jokes and giggles / Charles Keller; illustrated by
Dave Garbot.
      p.cm
  Includes index.
  ISBN 0-8069-2793-3
      1. Wit and humor, Juvenile. [1. Jokes.] I. Garbot, Dave,
ill. II. Title.
  PN6163. K429 2001
  818'.5402--dc21

                                    2001020197

10 9 8 7 6 5 4 3 2 1

Published by Sterling Publishing Company, Inc.
387 Park Avenue South, New York, N.Y. 10016
© 2001 by Charles Keller
Distributed in Canada by Sterling Publishing
 % Canadian Manda Group,
  One Atlantic Avenue, Suite 105
  Toronto, Ontario, Canada M6K 3E7
Distributed in Great Britain and Europe by Chris Lloyd
  463 Ashley Road, Parkstone, Poole,
  Dorset, BH14 0AX, England
Distributed in Australia by Capricorn Link (Australia) Pty Ltd.
  P.O. Box 6651, Baulkham Hills, Business Centre,
  NSW 2153, Australia

Sterling ISBN 0-8069-2793-3

Contents

1. Going Bananas

BOY: Lady, if you give me a dollar my brother will imitate a chicken.

LADY: What will he do—cackle?

BOY: No, he won't do a cheap trick like that. He'll eat a worm.

"I finally got my little brother to stop biting his nails."

"How?"

"I made him wear shoes."

SISTER: Mom wants you to come in and fix dinner.

BROTHER: Why, is it broken?

PATIENT: Doc, remember that bottle of pills you gave me to make me strong?

DOCTOR: Yes, I do.

PATIENT: I can't get the cap off the bottle.

CLIENT: Doctor, how much would you charge to do plastic surgery on my nose?

DOCTOR: A thousand dollars.

CLIENT: Anything cheaper?

DOCTOR: You could try walking into a lamppost.

PATIENT: Doctor, what should I take for a splitting headache?

DOCTOR: Have you tried glue?

PATIENT: Doctor, can you help me? It's my hearing. I can't even hear myself cough.

DOCTOR: Have this prescription filled.

PATIENT: Will it improve my hearing?

DOCTOR: No, but it will help you cough better.

WARPED WISE MAN

Keep smiling—it makes the grown-ups wonder what you've been up to.

PHYSICIAN: Take this medicine after every meal.
PATIENT: But doc, I haven't eaten in four days.
PHYSICIAN: Good. The medicine will last longer.

"Be careful with that cold. Sneeze the other way."
  "I don't know any other way."

CUSTOMER: Waiter, there's a fly in my soup.
WAITER: Sorry, sir, did you order without?

DINER: What's that fly doing in my alphabet soup?
WAITER: Trying to learn to read.

PATRON: There's a dragonfly in my soup.
WAITER: That's the cook. The last customer was a
  witch doctor.

DINER: Waiter, there's a water bug in my soup.
WAITER: Yes, sir, I know. If you throw that
particular one a pea, he'll play water polo.

HARVE: Well, plan A failed. Is plan B any good?
MARV: If plan B were any good, we would have
called it plan A.

Show me someone who lets a smile be his umbrella
and I'll show you someone with a mouth full of rain.

BOSS: What do you mean you were a big gun in
industry?
JOB APPLICANT: I've been fired a dozen times.

TEACHER: What do you call a person who eats only vegetables?
PUPIL: A vegetarian.

TEACHER: What do you call someone who eats people?
PUPIL: A humanitarian.

TEACHER: Michael, what kind of birds are found in captivity?
MICHAEL: Jailbirds.

MASKED MAN: Do you have flowers for all occasions?
FLORIST: Yes, we do. What's the occasion?
MASKED MAN: This is a stickup.

LADY (*at florist*): I want a dozen roses for my daughter's coming-out party.
FLORIST: It's none of my business, but what was she put away for?

FIRST BURGLAR: I think I need glasses.
SECOND BURGLAR: What makes you think so?
FIRST BURGLAR: On my last job I started to turn the knobs on the safe and the stereo began to play.

"My brother is so dumb."
    "How dumb is he?"
    "He got a pair of water skis for his birthday. Now he's looking for a lake with a hill in it."

SHIP'S CAPTAIN: Quick, operator! Get me an SOS!
OPERATOR: Sure, how do you spell it?

The captain of a sinking ship called the passengers and crew of the ship together and asked: "Is there anyone here who can pray?"

One passenger said, "I pray all the time."

"That's great," said the captain, "because we're short one life preserver."

TEACHER: Now if you bought ten apples for ten cents, what would each one be?
STUDENT: Rotten—at that price they'd have to be.

☆ NEWS BULLETIN ☆

A supermarket was robbed last night of 30 sacks of carrots and a bushel of garlic. Police are on the look-out for rabbits with bad breath.

Did you hear about the thief who stole a truck full of elastic? He was put away for a long stretch.

"I keep thinking today is Monday."
  "Today is Monday."
  "I know, that's why I keep thinking it."

"Do you have any superstitions?"
  "No, I think it's bad luck to have superstitions."

SPOOK: What's the only time a ghost can build a snowman?
LUKE: When?
SPOOK: In the dead of winter.

Daffynition

Boo-boo—what two ghosts say when they meet

Two men were arguing about the length of a pole. A passerby heard them. "Why don't you just lay it down on the ground and measure it?"
  "We want to know how high it is, not how long."

"Fred called me a dumbbell."

"You don't have to take that! Make him prove it."

"Remember that piano stool you sold me?"

"Yes."

"Well I twisted it in all directions and still can't get a note out of it."

What makes opening a piano so difficult?

The keys are on the inside.

MAN: Have you got something to cure fleas on a dog?

PET SHOP OWNER: I don't know. What's wrong with the fleas?

RICKY: Does your dog have a license?

DICKY: No, I don't let him drive.

"Did you tell me your dog's bark is worse than his bite?"

"Yes, why?"

"Then don't let him bark—he just bit me."

VISITOR: Does your dog bite strangers?

HOME OWNER: Only when he doesn't know them.

2. Off the Wall

What do you call a dinosaur that's never late?
Prontosaurus.

What do you call dinosaurs who are always walking in mud?
Brown-toe saurus.

ERNIE: I heard your father was a conductor. Was he a railroad or an orchestra conductor?
BERNIE: Neither, he was struck by lightning.

"I was at the mall yesterday on an escalator and there was a power failure."

"So?"

"I was stuck for hours."

Silly Billy mislaid his umbrella and went from store to store looking for it. When he finally found it he was jubilant. "You are the only honest store in town," he told the shopkeeper. "All the others denied having it."

"Mom, you know that vase that's been handed down from generation to generation?"

"Yes."

"Well, this generation dropped it."

APPLIANCE STORE CLERK: May I interest you in a new freezer?

LADY: No, I can't afford it.

CLERK: It will pay for itself in no time.

LADY: Okay, as soon as it does, send it over.

MOTHER: Why don't you let your little brother play with your marbles if he wants to?

BOY: But, Mom, he wants to keep them.

MOTHER: I'm sure he doesn't want to.

BOY: Well, he's swallowed two already.

WIFE: Why didn't you get the cat fixed?

HUSBAND: It wasn't broken.

"Why are you staring at me?"

"I'm sorry. But if it wasn't for the mustache you'd look just like my wife."

"But I don't have a mustache."

"I know. But my wife does."

TRAFFIC COP: Sir, you were going seventy miles an hour.

MAN: Isn't that amazing? And I just learned to drive yesterday!

HIGHWAY PATROLMAN: You were going seventy miles per hour.

SPEEDER: I was only following the signs.

PATROLMAN: That's the number of the highway.

SPEEDER: It is? I'm glad you didn't stop me on I-95.

SPEEDER: I didn't hear your siren.
COP: Of course not. You already passed the sound
   barrier.

POLICEMAN: When I saw you drive by, I thought
   you were pushing at least sixty.
WOMAN: Don't be rude, officer. I'm only forty-five.

PATRON: Why is your thumb in my soup?
WAITER: How else can I tell if it's hot?

CUSTOMER: Look at this chicken. It's nothing but
   skin and bones.
WAITER: Yes, sir. Would you like the feathers, too?

"Waiter, is this dish chili?"
    "Of course! I just took it out of the refrigerator."

MAN: I'd like a glass of ginger ale.
COUNTERPERSON: Pale?
MAN: No, a glass will be enough.

SHE: Am I the first girl you ever kissed?
HE: Now that you mention it, your face is familiar.

YOUNG LADY: I wouldn't marry you if you were the
    last person on earth.
YOUNG MAN: If I were, you wouldn't be here.

YOUNG MAN: Miss, would you go out with me
    tonight?
YOUNG LADY: I don't go out with perfect strangers.
YOUNG MAN: I never said I was perfect.

GOLFER: Notice the improvement since last year?
CADDY: Yes, you had your clubs shined, didn't you?

Brenda and Ruth were playing golf when a bird
flew overhead.
    Brenda said. "Look at that lovely swan."
    Ruth replied, "It was a duck."
    "It was a swan," said Brenda.
    Just then a golf ball was hit in their direction.
"Duck!" shouted Ruth.
    "Swan!" screamed Brenda.
    "Ka-bonk!" went the golf ball.

WARPED WISE MAN

Golf is no longer a rich man's sport. There are millions of poor players.

MAN: I'd like to buy a dozen golf balls.
CLERK: Do you want them gift wrapped?
MAN: No, I'll drive them home.

"When I was a child my nurse dropped me a lot."
   "What did your mother do?"
   "She got me a shorter nurse."

GIRL: Mom, is it true that people come from dust?
MOTHER: In a way, yes.
GIRL: And do they go back to dust?
MOTHER: Yes, they do.
GIRL: Well, I looked under the bed and someone is either coming or going.

MOTHER: The recipe for the cake says that you should separate two eggs. Did you do that?
YOUNG GIRL: Yes, Mom, I sure did. I put one in the living room and the other in the bedroom.

"I've been cooking for years."
   "Then I guess dinner must be ready now."

"Did you finish first in the pie-eating contest?"
  "No, I finished sickened."

MOTHER: Why did you come home at 3 a.m.?
DAUGHTER: You told me to come home early.

"Are you sure your mother won't mind me sailing
my boat in your bathtub?"
  "No, she can always slide to the other side."

DOCTOR: I have good news and bad news for you.
PATIENT: Give me the good news first.
DOCTOR: You're going to have a fatal disease
  named after you.

DOCTOR: Do you smoke or drink?
PATIENT: I didn't know I had a choice.

PATIENT: What should I do? I have water on the
knee.
DOCTOR: Wear pumps.

"My girlfriend won't talk to me since I took her
horseback riding."
"She could be sore about something."

BOY: Mom, Uncle Charlie took me to the zoo this
afternoon.
MOTHER: That's nice. Did you have a good time?
BOY: Yes, and one of the animals came in first and
paid twenty dollars.

HORSE: Does that bridle bother you?
PONY: Not a bit.

"A funny thing happened at the racetrack
yesterday. I bent down to tie my shoe when some
nearsighted jockey dropped a saddle on my back."
   "What did you do?"
   "What could I do? I ran the best race I could and
came in third."

"Where did you learn to swim?"
   "In the water."

"I once lived on water for two years."
   "When was that?"
   "When I was in the navy."

NAVY RECRUITER: Do you know how to swim?
RECRUIT: Why, aren't there enough ships?

"How did the witch get around when her
broomstick broke?"
   "She witchhiked."

"Did you know John has a glass eye?"
   "Did he tell you that?"
   "No, it came out in the conversation."

"Dad, what is a vacuum?"
   "Son, a vacuum is a void."
   "I know, but what does the void mean?"

3. Mirthquakes

"What do you do for a living?"
  "I'm a pilot."
  "Oh, do you fly airplanes?"
  "No, I work in an office with lots of paperwork. I pile it here and I pile it there."

FOREMAN: Why are you quitting this job?
WORKER: Oh, I don't mind smashing up roads with a jackhammer all day, but the guy who works with me hums constantly.

IGGY: Last night I heard you ran into a tree with your parent's car.
ZIGGY: It wasn't my fault. I honked my horn but the tree wouldn't get out of the way.

"How did you win the good driver's award?"
    "I was wreckless."

GIRL: I bumped into Joan today.
FRIEND: Was she glad to see you?
GIRL: Not really, we were in our cars at the time.

PROFESSOR: What law did Newton discover?
STUDENT: The bigger they are, the harder they fall.

DAUGHTER: Mom, can I join the track team?
MOM: Run that by me again.

"Are you still taking scuba diving lessons?"
    "No, I quit before I got in too deep."

"Can you ice skate?"
    "I don't know. I can't stand up long enough to find out."

FOREMAN: Do you think you're fit for hard labor?
APPLICANT: Some of the best judges in the country thought so.

"Mom, I want to be a baker."
    "Well, that takes the cake!"

"Did you hear about the person who decided to become a trapeze artist?"

"Everyone said it was high time."

DICK: Where have you been for the last four years?
JANE: I've been at college taking medicine.
DICK: And did you finally get well?

Duffy was baking a cake and suddenly ran away. Why did he do that?

It said on the recipe: "Break an egg and beat it."

"Will the band play anything I want them to?"

"Certainly, sir."

"Well, have them play cards."

"Where did Billy go?"

"He's round out front."

"I know what he looks like, just tell me where he went."

"So Joe was the life of the party?"

"Yeah, he was the only one who could talk louder than the music."

DOCTOR: Do you drink plenty of liquids?
PATIENT: That's all I drink.

DING: I opened a new business. I started making lamps out of vegetables.
DONG: What are they for?
DING: People on a light diet.

CUSTOMER: I'd like a cup of coffee.

FRIEND: I'd like one, too, and make sure it's in a clean cup.

WAITRESS (*bringing back the coffees*): Okay, which one of you ordered the clean cup?

PSYCHIATRIST: I wouldn't worry too much about your son making mud pies.

MOTHER: But, I do worry and so does his wife.

WOMAN: Do you have any grandchildren?

ELDERLY WOMAN: No, all my children are ordinary.

MAGICIAN (*in a restaurant*): That rabbit stew you served me tasted horrible. I'll never come here again.

WAITER: Well, that's the first time a rabbit made a magician disappear.

CUSTOMER: Waiter, I find that I have just enough money to pay for this dinner but nothing left to leave you a tip.

WAITER: Let me add up that check again.

FIRST MONKEY: I'm hungry.

SECOND MONKEY: Well, there's plenty of hamburger meat. Why don't you make yourself a hamburger?

FIRST MONKEY: How can I make a hamburger?

SECOND MONKEY: Just stick it on the gorilla.

A man walks into the doctor's office with french fries in one ear and a hot dog in the other. He says, "I'm not feeling well. Can you help me?"

"Well, I can tell you one thing," says the doctor. "You haven't been eating right."

"My grandma fell down the stairs."

"Cellar?"

"No, I think she can be repaired."

"I hear your brother fell into an upholstery machine."

"Yes, but he's fully recovered now."

27

"My uncle was on a quiz show and won a trip to Australia."

"Did he go?"

"Yes, five years ago. He's been trying to win a trip back ever since."

"To what do you attribute your old age, Grandpa?"

"I was born a long time ago."

What is the police officers' favorite board game?

Monopolice.

Who was the biggest horse thief of all time?

Al Ca-pony.

"My ancestry goes back thousands of years."

"I suppose you're going to tell me your family was in the ark with Noah."

"Certainly not. My people had a boat of their own."

Semi-conductor—a part-time orchestra leader

ANGRY WORKER: Hey, my paycheck is $50 short.
SUPERVISOR: That's because we overpaid you by $50 last week. Why didn't you complain then?
WORKER: I'm willing to overlook an occasional error, but this is two weeks in a row.

BOSS: Everything in this shop is electric.
WORKER: Well, the low salary gave me a shock.

LAWYER: Hello, I'd like to have some electrical work done. How much do you charge?
ELECTRICIAN: $75 an hour.
LAWYER: $75 an hour? I don't make that much as a lawyer.
ELECTRICIAN: Neither did I when I was a lawyer.

JUDGE: I'll give you a short sentence—ten years.
PRISONER: Ten years! That's not a short sentence!
JUDGE: Yes it is. Two words.

Who is the fastest criminal on two wheels?
A motor-psycho.

PARACHUTIST: What happens if my parachute doesn't open?
INSTRUCTOR: We'll take it back to the store and give you another one to replace it.

Workaholism by Anita Dayoff.

Never Say Good-bye by C.U. Latta

Crowd Control by General Panic

Amazing Facts by G. Willikers

"My name is Martin S. Johnson."
   "What's the S stand for?"
   "Nothing. The doctor dropped a noodle on my birth certificate."

"I wish we had brought the dresser to the airport with us."
   "Why?"
   "I left our tickets on it."

4. Hanky-Panky

"Did you hear what happened when they crossed an ostrich with a turkey to get bigger drumsticks?"

"No, what happened?"

"They got a scrawny bird that insisted on sticking its head in the mashed potatoes."

"My uncle taught his chickens to play baseball."

"That must be fascinating to watch."

"Not really, they keep hitting fowl balls."

SALESMAN: Why do you want to buy 5,000 roaches?

TENANT: I'm moving and the landlord insists that I leave the apartment as I found it.

"I come from a real small town."

"How small was it?"

"It was so small they had to close the zoo because the chicken died."

"How do you like your apartment as a whole?"

"As a hole, it's okay, as an apartment it's terrible."

"What a tumbledown shack. I wonder what is holding it together?"

"The termites are holding hands."

SON: Are bugs good to eat?

DAD: Let's not talk about it at the dinner table.

DAD (*after dinner*): Now, what's this about bugs?

SON: Nothing. There was one in your soup, but it's gone now.

WARPED WISE MAN

Show me a house divided
and I'll show you a
house that brings in
more rent.

The restaurant sign said, "We Fought the Roaches,"
so a diner went in and ordered soup: "Waiter, there's
a roach in my soup. The sign said you fought the
roaches."

"It didn't say we won."

YOUNG CENTIPEDE: A big insect stepped on one of
my feet.
MOTHER CENTIPEDE: I'll rub it and make it better.
Which foot is it?
YOUNG CENTIPEDE: I don't know. I can only count
to ten.

What do karate and judo experts eat before a
match?
Kung food.

"Are you a runner yet?"
"No, but I'm making great strides."

"Would you rather lose your money or your life?"
"My life. I need my money for my old age."

33

How did the karate student feel about failing the test?

He could kick himself.

Why couldn't the boxer start a fire?
Because he lost all his matches.

"I commute to work every day by train. I live in Fishhook."

"Fishhook? Where's that?"

"At the end of the line."

CUSTOMER (*to paper boy*): Do you mind if I pay you in pennies?

PAPER BOY: Of course not. Do you mind if I deliver your paper one page at a time?

"Since I lost my money one-half of my friends don't know me anymore."

"And the other half?"

"They don't know I lost it yet."

RANCHER: Why are you staring at that piece of rope?

SECOND RANCHER: I'm not sure if I found a piece of rope or lost a horse.

COWBOY: You're putting your saddle on backwards.

DUDE: How can you tell? You don't know which way I'm going.

"Did you hear about the actress who fell off her seven-inch heels?"

"Was she hurt?"

"No, her eyelashes broke her fall."

The Last Supper by M.T. Potts

Fast Food by Eaton Run

The Bee Hive by I. Ben Stung

Turn Off the Light by Les Watts

MOTHER: Let's buy Junior a bike.
FATHER: Do you think it will improve his behavior?
MOTHER: No, but at least he'll spread it around the
 neighborhood.

"Are you going to use your bike today?"
 "Yes, I'm sorry."
 "Good! Then you won't be using your car. May I
borrow it?"

MAN AT MOVIE THEATER: You advertise "Popular
 Prices" and yet you charge $7 to see a movie. Do
 you call that a popular price?
CASHIER: We like it.

USHER: How far down do you want to sit?
LADY: All the way, I'm tired.

"Can't you play tennis without making so much noise?"

"Don't be silly, you can't play tennis without raising a racket."

Daffynition

Europe—what the umpire says
when it's your turn to bat

CUSTOMER: I'd like to return this baseball bat.
SPORTS STORE CLERK: What's wrong with it?
CUSTOMER: Every time I've been to bat with it I
   strike out.

"I stopped at a very exclusive hotel."

"How exclusive was it?"

"It was so exclusive that room service had an unlisted number."

"Hello, front desk."

"How much do you charge for a room?"

"Our rates start at $50 a day."

"Do you take children?"

"No sir, only cash and credit cards."

JUDGE: Don't you know that crime doesn't pay?
CRIMINAL: Yes, but the hours are good.

"There is a mouse in the kitchen."

"Leave it. Mice are supposed to be lucky."

"This one certainly is. It ate your lunch."

"If your father brought your mother a mink, why is she so angry?"

"She has to clean the cage."

ZOOKEEPER (*on the phone*): We've got a problem here at the zoo, sir. One of the leopards escaped from its cage and is now just ten feet from me. What should I do?

HEAD OF THE ZOO: Tranquilize it on the spot.

ZOOKEEPER: Which one?

JUDGE: Guilty or not guilty?

DEFENDANT: I don't know. I haven't heard the evidence yet.

What do you call the factory where computers are made?

Apple source.

What kind of hardware is used on the bottom of the sea?

Clam-puters.

(*A man falls down a flight of stairs and someone rushes up to him.*)

PERSON: Did you miss a step?

MAN: No, I hit every one of them.

PATRON: Waiter, there's a fly in my soup.
WAITER: Quick! Throw him some water wings!

CUSTOMER: Waiter, there's a fly drowning in my
   soup.
WAITER: Quick! Get a lifeguard.

CUSTOMER: Waiter, there's a fly in my soup.
WAITER: Wait a minute, I'll get you a fork.

PATIENT: Doctor, what should I do with these little
   green men crawling all over my arms?
DOCTOR: I don't know, but don't give any to me.

PSYCHIATRIST: Why do you now say you are George Washington? On your last visit here you said you were Napoleon Bonaparte.

PATIENT: Yes, but that was by my first mother.

PATIENT: I'm always dizzy for half an hour after I get up in the morning.

DOCTOR: Well, try getting up half an hour later.

PATIENT: Doc, you've got to help me. I snore so loudly that I wake myself up.

DOCTOR: In that case, sleep in another room.

PATIENT: Doctor, I'm feeling a bit schizophrenic.

DOCTOR: That makes four of us.

5. In One Ear

BOY: Mom, there's a man at the door with a bill.
MOTHER: Don't be silly, it must be a duck with a
  hat on.

BOY: There's a woman outside who's collecting for
  the new church extension.
FATHER: Give her a brick.

MOTHER: Why is your little brother crying?
SON: Because I won't give him my piece of cake.
MOTHER: Is his piece gone?
SON: Yes, he cried when I ate that, too.

"I heard your sister had a new baby."

"Yes, but they didn't say what sex it was, so I don't know if I'm an uncle or an aunt."

"My sister is black-and-blue because she puts on cold cream, wrinkle cream, and hair cream every night."

"But why does that make her black-and-blue?"

"She keeps slipping out of bed."

BOY: Dad, there's a man at the door with a drum.

DAD: Tell him to beat it.

Do morticians have to study anatomy?

Of corpse.

A man rushed into an elevator. "Tenth floor," he shouted.

"But there are only six floors in this building," said the operator.

"Okay, then," replied the man. "Take me to the sixth floor and I'll walk the rest of the way."

WARPED WISE MAN

If at first you do succeed, try to hide your astonishment.

"My uncle got a new job at the circus. He's shot out of a cannon."

"Wow! How does he withstand the shock?"

"I really don't know. We haven't found him yet."

"I bought a book on bodybuilding, and I've been working hard on the exercises for three months."

"Is it having any effect?"

"It certainly is. Now I can lift the book."

Two men were walking along and one of them fell into a well. The other knew that he couldn't swim, so he called down to him, "Is the well empty?"

The call came back from below: "No, I'm in it!"

"My uncle went hunting and didn't have a hunting license. He caught a bear. The game warden asked him for his license, so thinking he was clever, he showed him his marriage license."

"What happened?"

"He had to marry the bear."

SIGN: Beware of the grizzlies.
CAMPER: I'll bear that in mind.

(A lion and a cheetah were playing cards.)
LION: I know why I can't beat you. You're a cheater.
CHEETAH: Well, you're a lion.

A group of hikers were helplessly lost. They demanded an explanation from their guide. "We thought you were the best guide in Maine."

"I am," replied the guide, "but I think we're in Canada."

TROOP LEADER: One of the things you'll learn as scouts is how to make fires out of doors.
SCOUT: That sounds like fun—where do you get all the doors from?

FOREST WARDEN: Which of you saw this rare tree get cut down?
CAMPER: Only the chain saw.

HECKLE: How do you like that secondhand clock you bought?
JECKLE: It's great! It saves me so much time! It does an hour in fifty minutes.

"So your uncle is dead. Did he leave you much in his will?"

"Only an old clock."

"Then you won't have too much trouble winding up the estate."

DONALD: So it's Thanksgiving. What have I got to be thankful for? I can't even pay my credit card bills.
RONALD: Be thankful you're not one of your credit card companies.

ASTRONAUT: I just got back from the moon and it's a great, big ball of cheese.
COMMANDER: Why did you come back?
ASTRONAUT: To get some crackers.

FIRST ASTRONAUT: What has eight eyes, ten arms, and is green all over?
SECOND ASTRONAUT: I don't know. What?
FIRST ASTRONAUT: I don't know either. But it's looking in our window.

"I'm sorry you fell down a flight of stairs."
   "That's all right. I had to come down anyway."

ZOO VISITOR: I wonder what that tiger would say if it could talk?
ZOOKEEPER: It would probably say, "I beg your pardon, sir, but I'm a leopard."

TEACHER: How do you spell wrong?
STUDENT: R-O-N-G.
TEACHER: That's wrong.
STUDENT: That's what you asked for.

HISTORY TEACHER: Name the Tudor kings and queens of England.
BETTY: First there was Henry the Seventh, then Henry the Eighth and then Edward the Sixth and then Mary.
TEACHER: Correct, and who came after Mary?
BETTY: Er...the little lamb?

"How did you smash up your car so badly?"
   "I hit a pedestrian."
   "That wrecked your car like that?"
   "He was on a bus."

TEACHER: Gabriel, why are you late for school?
GABRIEL: I must have over-washed.

"Did you hear about the man who built a moped with wooden wheels and a wooden engine?"
   "What happened to it?"
   "Wooden go."

47

"It's outrageous that this truck driver is charging us $50 for towing us two miles."

"Don't worry. He's earning it. I have the brakes on."

"I just got rid of my set of drums as a down payment on a car."

"I didn't know they accepted things like that as a down payment."

"Well, in my case it was different. The car dealer was my next door neighbor."

TAXI DRIVER: That will be three-fifty, please.
FARE: I'm a little short of money. Could you back up to two-seventy-five?

A man walked into a restaurant that boasted it could supply any dish that the customer ordered.

"I'll have an elephant sandwich with ketchup," he said

The waiter returned a few minutes later empty-handed. "I'm sorry, sir, we've run out of ketchup."

WAITER: You ought to give me a tip. Why, every champion cheapskate that comes into this restaurant gives me a quarter.
CUSTOMER: Meet the new champ.

CUSTOMER: May I have a table for dinner?
WAITER: Yes, sir—roasted, boiled, or fried?

6. Caught Red-Handed

"My dad thinks that old Mr. Jones down the block is a vampire."

"What makes him think that?"

"I heard him telling Mom that Mr. Jones is a pain in the neck."

LITTLE KID: Are you a pirate?

PIRATE: Yes, I am.

LITTLE KID: I thought all pirates had a ring in their ear.

PIRATE: That's funny. I don't hear anything.

PATIENT: Doc, do you remember last year you told me to stay away from dampness if I wanted my arthritis to get better.

DOCTOR: Yes, I do.

PATIENT: Well, it's better. Is it all right if I take a shower now?

Did you hear the joke about the quicksand? It takes a long time to sink in.

"How did you get those freckles on your face?"
    "I sunbathe through a screen door."

WARPED WISE MAN

A day without sun-shine is like night.

"The new lion trainer at the circus was mauled by one of the lions."
    "Was he clawed?"
    "I don't know his name—we weren't introduced."

"I always say people should sleep with their windows open."
    "Oh, you're a doctor, are you?"
    "No, a burglar."

FATHER: Son, I'm a self-made man.

SON: That's what I like about you, Dad. You always take the blame for everything.

SON: Dad, there's a man at the door with a funny face.

FATHER: Tell him you've already got one.

TOURIST: Excuse me, but how far is it to Smithville?

COUNTRY BOY: It's 5,000 miles in the direction you're heading in your car, but only five miles if you turn around and go the other way.

PATIENT: If I take these pills, will I get better?

DOCTOR: Well, let's put it this way—none of my patients ever came back for more.

WOMAN: My doctor put me on a diet of corn and vegetable oils.

OTHER WOMAN: Does it work?

WOMAN: I'm not losing any weight, but I don't squeak anymore.

"Have you considered early retirement?"

"Oh yes, I'm always in bed by ten."

"I can't believe it. My wallet was stolen from right under my nose!"

"Gee, it probably would have been safer if it was in your pants pocket."

HOLDUP MAN: Stick 'em up!

VICTIM: You're wasting your time. I'm broke. I haven't had more than a dollar in my pocket in months.

HOLDUP MAN: You think you've got it tough. You don't know what tough is. I haven't been able to afford gas for the getaway car for over a year.

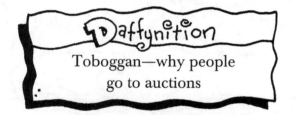

Daffynition

Toboggan—why people
go to auctions

FARMER: That horse you sold me yesterday was blind.

HORSE TRADER: Well, I told you he didn't look so good.

VISITOR: With so many cows, how can you tell which is which?

FARMER: I've been milking them so long I can tell one from the udder.

"I packed my own lunch today."
  "What did you bring?"
  "Chocolate soup."
  "Chocolate soup? What's that?"
  "Well, this morning it was ice cream."

MAN: You know that girl I married that I met
  through a personal ad in the newspaper?
FRIEND: What about her?
MAN: There's a problem. Every time I pick up the
  newspaper she thinks I'm cheating on her.

A couple walked down the street and stopped in front of a jewelry store.

"I love that diamond pin in the window," she said.

He took a brick out of his pocket, broke the window, and handed her the pin.

They walked a little farther and came to another jewelry store.

She said, "I love that pair of diamond earrings."

He took another brick out of his pocket and broke the window and handed her the earrings.

They walked a little farther and reached a third jewelry store. She said, "I love that diamond ring."

He turned to her and said, "What is this? You think I'm made of bricks?"

HUSBAND: I'll make dinner. Guests will be dropping over.
WIFE: They will if they eat your dinner.

PIANO PLAYER: Do you think I have a gift for playing?
LISTENER: No, but I'll give you one for stopping.

LOVE-STRUCK YOUTH: For you I could climb the highest mountain, swim the deepest river, and cross the driest desert.
GIRL: Oh, that's so romantic. Are we still on for the picnic on Saturday?
BOY: Sure, if it doesn't rain.

"What did you think about the marriage of the model and the fashion designer?"

"They are well suited."

"Are you still dating the librarian?"

"No, I closed the book on that relationship."

MOTHER: Did your boyfriend enjoy the dinner you made him last night?

DAUGHTER: I guess so. He said he hasn't been able to eat anything since.

"Give me a glass of water."

"Say 'please.'"

"Please what?"

"Please give me a glass of water."

"I asked you first."

"I was out with a nurse last night."

"Well, if you behave, maybe they'll let you out without one."

BOYFRIEND: Darling, I'm burning with love for you.
GIRLFRIEND: Oh, don't make a fuel of yourself.

"I have this violin in my house that was made in 1789."

"Oh, did you buy it new?"

Did you hear about the trombone player who just let things slide?

"I'm sorry to hear that your factory burned down. What did you manufacture?"

"Fire extinguishers."

FIRST CAT: How did you make out at the milk-drinking contest?
SECOND CAT: Oh, I won by six laps.

DOG OWNER: I'd like to buy a license for my dog.
CLERK: Certainly. Name please?
DOG OWNER: Spot.

"What's your dog's name?"
"I don't know. He won't tell me."

Did you hear about the man who was so grouchy that his dog put up a sign that said, "Beware of Owner."

WAITER: You can have anything you see on the menu.
DINER: Well, how about dirty fingerprints, grease stains, and gravy?

"Waiter, I'll have the spaghetti. Will it be long?"
"I don't know. I never measured it."

"Waiter, look at this chicken you served me. One leg is shorter than the other."
"Were you planning to eat it or dance with it?"

WOMAN: What's this fly doing in my ice cream?
WAITER: Probably cooling off. It gets pretty hot in the kitchen.

7. Thanks, but No, Thanks

CUSTOMER: I'd like a pair of stockings for my wife.
CLERK: Sheer?
CUSTOMER: No, she's home.

CUSTOMER: Four bars of soap, please.
CLERK: Scented?
CUSTOMER: No, I'll take them with me.

LADY IN PET STORE: Have you got any kittens going cheap?
CLERK: No, ma'am. All our kittens go "meow."

CUSTOMER: Those children's pants you sold me last week were no good. I washed them once and they shrunk so much my child can hardly walk. What should I do?

STORE CLERK: Try washing your son. Maybe he'll shrink too.

HILLBILLY: What are those things?

STOREKEEPER: They're pajamas. You wear them at night. Would you like to buy a pair?

HILLBILLY: Nope. Don't go no place at night except to bed.

OFFICE MANAGER: Are you good at filing?

YOUNG LADY: Yes, on my last job I filed seven hours a day. If you don't believe me, look at my nails.

BOSS: I'm sorry, but I can't give you a job. I just haven't got enough work to keep you busy.

APPLICANT: You'd be surprised at how little it takes to keep me busy.

DOLLY: Next week I'm going to Las Vegas to get a job as a chorus girl.

MOLLY: There's no use going there unless you have good legs.

DOLLY: Why? Don't they have elevators?

MAN (*jumping into a cab*): Follow the car in front.

CABBIE: I have to. It's towing us.

"Hey, cabbie ! How much will you charge to take me to the station?"

"Five bucks."

"And how much for my suitcase?"

"No charge for the suitcase."

"Okay, take the suitcase. I'll walk."

CAR DEALER: This car had just one careful owner.

BUYER: But look at it. It's a wreck!

CAR DEALER: Well, the other five owners weren't so careful.

WARPED WISE MAN

It takes a thousand nuts and bolts to put a car together, but just one nut to scatter it all over the road.

DOCTOR: Cheer up. I have the same ailment as you.

PATIENT: Yes, but you've got a different doctor.

DOCTOR: You really need glasses.

PATIENT: I'm already wearing glasses.

DOCTOR: In that case, I need glasses.

"When my grandfather was in India he chased elephants on horseback."

"No kidding. I didn't know elephants could ride horses."

"I got a new job restoring antiques."
   "That's interesting. Where do you work?"
   "At the beauty clinic."

"Mom, there's a man collecting for the old folks' home. Should I give him Grandma?"

LADY TO BEGGAR: Why don't you get a job?
BEGGAR: Actually, I'm an author. I once wrote a
   book entitled "One Hundred Ways to Make
   Money."
LADY: Then why are you begging?
BEGGAR: It's one of the ways.

GRANDMA: Remember my motto. Never put off till tomorrow what you can do today.

GRANDDAUGHTER: Okay, Grandma, that makes sense. We'd better eat the rest of the cake.

PANHANDLER: Lady, could you help me out? I've asked for money, begged for money, cried for money...

LADY: Why don't you work for money?

PANHANDLER: I'm going through the alphabet and I haven't gotten to W yet.

Did you hear about the author who made a fortune because he was in the write business?

CAVE MAN ONE: Look, I invented the light bulb.
CAVE MAN TWO: Don't be silly. We haven't
  discovered electricity yet.

Did you hear about the cannibal wedding party?
They toasted the bride and groom.

A visitor looked at amazement as he saw a friend's
child hammering nails into the house's expensive
furniture. "Don't you find it expensive to have your
child playing games like that?"
  "Not really. I get the nails wholesale."

MAN IN HARDWARE STORE: Have you got long nails?
CLERK: Yes, sir.
MAN: Could you scratch my back for me, please?

"Are you going to build a bookcase?"
   "No, I've shelved that project."

"For my hobby I kill flies with a bow and arrow."
   "Isn't that sort of messy?"
   "No, I only aim at the legs."

"Did you know that you have one black and one
white sock on?"
   "That's funny. I have another pair home just like
that."

NEIGHBOR: How many children in your family, little
   boy?
BOY: Nine.
NEIGHBOR: Gee, that must cost your family a fortune.
BOY: We don't rent them, we just raise them.

"I can't come to your party tonight. I'm going to
see *Romeo and Juliet.*"
   "That's okay, bring them along. The more the
merrier."

FIRST OCTOPUS: I don't know what to buy my
   husband for Christmas.
SECOND OCTOPUS: Do what I did. Get him four
   pairs of gloves.

"Have you ever seen a fish cry?"
"No, but I've seen a whale blubber."

"Why don't you like masseurs?"
"They rub me the wrong way."

Did you hear about the man who got a bad haircut?
He kept it under his hat.

"Have you any invisible ink?"
"Certainly, sir. What color?"

WIT: Why did the man go crazy in the clothing
   store ?
DIM: I don't know.
WIT: He heard it was a good place to have a fit.

8. Facing the Music

What monster is big and gray and wears a mask?
The Elephant-om of the Opera.

Did you hear about the composer who only worked in bed? He composed sheet music.

What famous filmmaker lived in a safe?
Vault Disney.

"How's the new chef doing?"
"Great, she's really cooking!"

What did they call MTV when all the VJs went out on strike?

Empty-V.

THEO: What happened when the student chef made a mess of an omelet in cooking class?
DORA: What happened?
THEO: He was eggs-spelled.

CUSTOMER: What flavor ice cream do you have?
WAITRESS (*whispering*): We have vanilla, chocolate, and strawberry.
CUSTOMER: Do you have laryngitis?
WAITRESS: No, just vanilla, chocolate, and strawberry.

WAITER: May I help you with your soup?
DINER: What do you mean?
WAITER: Well, from the sound, I thought you might like me to drag you ashore.

CUSTOMER: Waiter, I've only got one piece of meat.
WAITER: Just a minute, sir. I'll cut it for you.

CUSTOMER: Hey, waiter!
WAITER: We usually don't serve that, but in your
    case I'll make an exception.

COP: Why did you steal everything from that store?
CROOK: The sign said "Take Out Only."

PATIENT: Doctor, I keep seeing spots.
DOCTOR: Have you seen a psychiatrist?
PATIENT: No, just spots.

"Doctor, remember you told me to eat lots of
carrots to improve my eyesight? Be like a rabbit,
you said."
    "Yes, I remember."
    "My eyesight improved, but I keep tripping over
my ears."

PATIENT: I've had this bad cough all week and it isn't getting better.

DOCTOR: Well, keep practicing.

LADY: I'd like to open a joint bank account.

TELLER: Who would you like to open it with?

LADY: Somebody who has a lot of money.

Show me someone with a gold tooth and I'll show you someone who puts his money where his mouth is.

"How did you get that rash on your head?"

"I bit myself."

"Come on, how could you bite yourself on the forehead?"

"I stood on a chair."

WARPED WISE MAN

A truly wise man never plays leapfrog with a unicorn.

PATTY: I've been playing the lottery for ten years now and never had a winner.

HATTIE: Then why don't you give it up?

PATTY: Are you nuts! And give up ten years of experience?

One student wanted to make sure he knew all the answers in his tests, so he wrote them all over his body. History was on his right leg, math was on his left arm—all over his body were answers. He wrote out so many answers, his skin graduated six months before he did.

ARTIST: I'll give you twenty dollars if you let me paint you. You wouldn't have to do anything for the money.
HILLBILLY: I wasn't thinking about the money. I was just wondering how I'd get the paint off after you finished.

VISITOR: How many sheep do you have?
SHEPHERD: Can't say exactly. Every time I start to count them I fall asleep.

Cattle Ranching by Brandon D. Bull

Bullfighting Mistakes by Gordon Bluddy

JUDGE: You are accused of shooting rabbits out of season. How do you plea?

HUNTER: Self-defense, your honor.

JUDGE: The court can produce a dozen witnesses who saw you rob the bank.

ROBBER: Big deal! I can bring in hundreds of people who didn't see it.

CONVICT'S WIFE (*on visiting day*): It's a shame you went on a hunger strike.

CONVICT: Why?

CONVICT'S WIFE: I put a file in your cake.

What happened when the hotel owner died under mysterious circumstances?

The police held an inn-quest.

BIFF: You must have paid the earth for that watch.

BOFF: Oh, does it look expensive?

BIFF: No, dirt cheap.

CUSTOMER: Look at that watch you sold me. It broke. You told me it would last a lifetime.
CLERK: Yeah, but you looked pretty sick the day you bought it.

"Did you see the eclipse of the moon last night?"
"No, it was so dark I couldn't see a thing."

Did you hear about the telephone operator who was arrested? The judge let her off the hook.

MAN: Doctor, is it okay to marry an octopus?

DOCTOR: Of course not.

MAN: One more thing. Do you know anybody who wants to buy eight engagement rings?

KID: Dad, is it true that an apple a day keeps the doctor away?

DAD: That's what they say.

KID: Well, give me an apple, quick! I've just broken the doctor's window!

How does a computer feel when it's overweight? *Disk-gusted.*

SURGEON: I have to bring this suit back. It's all
  wrong.
TAILOR: What's wrong with it?
SURGEON: I don't know. It was all right until I took
  out the stitches.

I stayed in a small village last summer. The
landlady kept animals. On the first day, one of the
chickens died, so we had chicken for dinner. On
the next day, one of the pigs died, so we had pork
chops. On the next day, her husband died—so I left
before dinner.

"Did you have a lot of money left at the end of
your vacation?"

  "No, but I had a lot of vacation left at the end of
my money."

☆ NEWS BULLETIN ☆

The meeting of the earthquake committee was
canceled after a motion from the floor.

9. Blockbusters

CUSTOMER: Give me something to eat and make it snappy.

WAITER: How about a crocodile sandwich?

LADY: I don't want this parrot you sold me last week. All it does is scream for whiskey and use the foulest language.

PET STORE OWNER: Don't be so critical, lady. Just be happy it doesn't gamble.

SILLY: Does your parrot talk?

SILLIER: He sure does. Since I bought him my phone bill tripled.

Daffynition

Polygon—what you say when
your parrot flies away

PIT: Last night I saw a robin at my favorite
restaurant.
PAT: He was probably there for the early-bird
  special.

CUSTOMER: Waiter, there's a little beetle in my soup.
WAITER: I'm sorry about that, sir, shall I exchange
  it for a bigger one?

CUSTOMER: Waiter, there's a dead bug in my soup.
WAITER: Yes, sir, they're not very good swimmers.

WAITER: Would you like an egg on toast?
CUSTOMER: Why, haven't you got any plates?

PSYCHIATRIST: As a new patient, why don't you start
  at the beginning?
PATIENT: Okay. In the beginning I created heaven
  and earth.

WIFE: My husband thinks he's a TV antenna,
  doctor.
DOCTOR: Now don't worry, I think I can cure him.
WIFE: I don't want him cured—I want him adjusted
  so that I can get Channel 4.

MAN: Why are you standing in the puddle?
FRIEND: It's my pills—they're to be taken in water, three times a day.

PATIENT: Doctor, I feel like a snail.
DOCTOR: You just need to come out of your shell.

"Mom, I took a splinter out of my hand with a pin."
   "A pin! Don't you know that can be dangerous?"
   "It's all right. It was a safety pin."

MOM: What are you doing?
SON: I'm washing myself.
MOM: Without soap and water?
SON: Haven't you heard of dry cleaning?

"No, you can't have any more ice cream. It's bad to go to bed with a full stomach."
   "But, Mom. I can sleep on my side, can't I?"

"Mom, isn't it dinner time yet?"
   "Not yet, dear."
   "Then my stomach must be fast."

VINNIE: What kind of vegetables do ghouls like best?
MINNIE: What kind?
VINNIE: Tomb-atoes.

What is an ape's favorite kind of cookie?
   Chocolate chimp.

What's Dracula's favorite kind of ice cream?
Blooderscotch.

What do monsters order in fast-food restaurants?
French frights.

"On your last trip to Paris, did you get any French francs?"
'Yes, but they're not as good our hot dogs."

"Hey, who do you think you're pushing?"
"I don't know—what's your name?"

WIFE: Why are you so nervous?
HUSBAND: I'm worried about our teenage son.
WIFE: Why? What does he have?
HUSBAND: His driver's license.

"What happened when you told your parents you wanted to be a rose gardener?"

"They nipped that idea in the bud."

DELIA: What happens when you call 116 for the police?
CELIA: I don't know.
DELIA: The police car comes to you upside down.

POLICEMAN: Where do you two live?

SUSPECT #1: No permanent address.

SUSPECT #2: I live in the apartment above his.

POLICE OFFICER: You are charged with having your
dog chase a man on a bicycle.

MAN: That's crazy. My dog doesn't even know how
to ride a bicycle.

DIT: The police are looking for a man with one eye
named Smith.

DOT: What's the other eye called?

PRISON WARDEN: For being such a bad prisoner, I'm going to put you on a diet of bread and water. How would you like that?

PRISONER: Make it whole wheat and Perrier.

POLICE DESK SERGEANT: Can I help you?

MAN: Yes, someone threw this dead fish into my front yard.

SERGEANT: Okay, sir. Come back in six months and if nobody claims it you can keep it.

NEW PRISONER: How long are you in for?

SECOND PRISONER: A hundred and twenty years.

NEW PRISONER: I'm in for a hundred and fifty. You better take the bed near the door because you'll be getting out first.

WARDEN: What do you want for your last meal?

CONDEMNED PRISONER: Watermelon.

WARDEN: There won't be any watermelon until next year.

PRISONER: I'll wait.

DR. WATSON: Holmes, what is your favorite tree?

SHERLOCK HOLMES: A lemon tree, my dear Watson.

ARMY COOK: Don't waste food like that. You should eat it. Don't you know the old saying "Food will win the war"?

SOLDIER: It sure would. But how are we going to get the enemy to eat it?

GAME WARDEN: There's no fishing allowed here.
BOY: I'm not fishing. I'm washing my pet worm.

A small boy was fishing through a small hole in the ice when a bigger boy came along and said: "You sure are dumb. If you catch a large fish you'll never be able to get him through this small hole."

The little boy responded: "No, you're the one who's dumb. If I catch a big fish it won't be able to pull me through this small hole."

SON: Can I have two pieces of cake?
MOM: Certainly, take this piece and cut it in half.

"Little girl, did you catch that big fish all by yourself?"

"No, a little worm helped me."

A woman walked into a music store and asked about a used piano, "This one here must be very old. The keys are all yellow."

"No, the piano isn't old," said the salesman. "It's just that the elephant was a heavy smoker."

WARPED WISE MAN

Be tolerant of those who disagree with you. After all, they're entitled to their stupid opinions.

"I went to the doctor to see if he could help me give up smoking."

"What did he say?"

"He suggested that every time I felt like a smoke, I should reach for a lollipop."

"Did it do any good?"

"No, I can't get the lollipop to light up."

10. Up the Creek

"My brother is in the hospital with spotted fever."

"Is it serious?"

"No, fortunately they spotted it in time."

"Doctor, I get pains in my chest every time I breathe."

"Well, don't breathe so much."

PATIENT: Doctor, I just swallowed a bone.

DOCTOR: Are you choking?

PATIENT: No, I'm serious.

"Dad, there's a man outside collecting for the new city pool."

"All right, give him a pail of water."

"I'll have to stop going to that psychiatrist. He told me I was in love with my handbag."

"That's ridiculous."

"I know. We're very fond of each other, but love?"

"That was nice to give your little brother the baseball cards for his birthday. But there's one problem—he can't read."

"That's okay, Mom. He can look at the pitchers."

WARPED WISE MAN

When things look black, send them to the laundry.

"After we'd been married two years, there was a patter of little feet."

"You had a baby?"

"No, mice."

PATIENT: Doctor, my tongue is always sticking out.

DOCTOR: Hold it a second, I've got some stamps to lick.

"Dad, do you like baked apples?

"Yes, son, why?"

"The orchard is on fire."

"I used to think I was a dog, but the doctor cured me."

"So you're all right now?"

"Yes, here—feel my nose."

DOCTOR: You need glasses.

PATIENT: How can you tell?

DOCTOR: I knew as soon as I saw you coming in through the window.

BESS: Did you know that China has a standing army of over two million men?

WES: They must be very short of chairs in China.

People who buy the new jogging machine
are getting a run for their money.

MOTHER: Why don't you play football with your
little brother?

BOY: He doesn't like it, Mom, and I'd rather have a
real football.

LITTLE ASHLEY: When I get older, I'm going to
marry the boy next door.

VISITOR: Why is that?

LITTLE ASHLEY: Cause I'm not allowed to cross the
street.

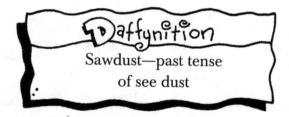

Daffynition

Sawdust—past tense
of see dust

AGENT: So you're a four-piece band, are you?

MUSICIAN: That's right, we know four pieces.

"How can you spot the owner of a shark in a pet
store?"

"How?"

"He's the one buying the two-mile leash."

"My cat got first prize at the bird show."
  "At the bird show? How did it do that?"
  "It ate the prize canary."

BIFF: What's good for fleas?
BOFF: How about dogs?

Show me a dog catcher and I'll show you a spot
remover.

CUSTOMER: I'll have a piece of pie, please.
WAITER: Anything with it?
CUSTOMER: If it's like the last time, better give me a
   hammer and chisel.

DINER: What do you call this?

WAITER: Cottage cheese, why?

DINER: I think I've just bitten off a piece of the door.

"Waiter, this salad is frozen solid."

"Yes, sir, it's the iceberg lettuce that does it."

CUSTOMER: Bring me a cup of coffee.

WAITER: I'm sorry, sir. We only have tea. The coffee is completely exhausted.

CUSTOMER: I'm not surprised. It's been weak for several days.

TEACHER: An apple comes under fruit, a potato comes under vegetables, so what does an egg come under?

STUDENT: A hen.

TEACHER: You're late again. What's the excuse this time?

BILLY: I ran so fast I didn't have time to think one up.

Did you hear the joke about the church bell? It's never been tolled.

MAN: I'd like to buy a new mattress.

FURNITURE CLERK: Would you like a spring mattress, sir?

MAN: No, I'd like one I can use all year round.

CUSTOMER: I want my money back! This bread is full of holes.
BAKER: Of course it is. It's hole-wheat bread.

LANA: I had to give up tap dancing.
DANA: Why?
LANA: I kept falling into the sink.

ACTOR: Perhaps you've seen me in the movie *Diner*?"
FRIEND: Did you have a big role?
ACTOR: No, just a muffin and coffee.

ANGRY CUSTOMER: Those safety matches you sold me won't strike.

STOREKEEPER: Well, you can't get much safer than that.

MAN: Why is that man hanging from the ceiling by one arm?

TAILOR: Oh, pay no attention to him. He thinks he's a light bulb.

MAN: Well, why don't you tell him he isn't?

TAILOR: What? And work in the dark?

ACTRESS: Do you think my latest movie will change people's lives?

CRITIC: It might—after all, your last movie changed two theaters into bowling alleys overnight.

"Can you see the movie screen?"
   "Yes."
   "Is your seat comfortable?"
   "Yes."
   "Are you in a draft?"
   "No."
   "Would you change seats with me?"

Did you hear about the thief who stole a truck full of elastic? He was put away for a long stretch.

CHIP: I'm a night watchman.

RIP: What do you watch?

CHIP: I don't know. It's so dark I can't see.

FOREMAN: Come on, get a move on with that bricklaying.

BRICKLAYER: Rome wasn't built in a day, you know.

FOREMAN: That's because I wasn't the foreman on the job.

Did you hear about the guy who slept in his car? He didn't want to walk in his sleep.

LADY (*on elevator*): I don't like the noises this old elevator is making. If the cables break, will we go up or down?

OPERATOR: That depends on what kind of life you've led.

POSTAL CLERK: Sorry, sir, but this package is too heavy. You have to put more stamps on it.

MAN: But that would only make it heavier.

CLOWN: Boss, the tent is on fire!

CIRCUS MANAGER: Quick, get the fire-eater!

Little Tommy was very well behaved, and every time he was good, his mother gave him a quarter and put it on his head. By the time he was eighteen he had $32,000, but he was only three feet tall.

Index

96